Harmony in Diversity

Lessons from World Cultures

Table of Contents

The beauty of the world lies in the diversity of its people.

Chapter 1. Introduction

Dive into a colorful mosaic of global cultures with our Special Report, "Harmony in Diversity: Lessons from World Cultures". This vibrant journey across continents will invigorate your spirit, ignite your curiosity, and inspire you with an appreciation for diversity. From the bustling markets of Marrakech to the peaceful temples of Kyoto, through the tribal dances of the Masai and the family gatherings of the Inuit people, we shine a light on the beauty and harmony that lives within our world's diversity. Uncover invaluable lessons unique to each culture, all the while discovering the unifying ties that make us all human. Pack your intellectual bags and be ready for an exciting cultural journey. This bright tapestry of stories, experiences, and wisdom awaits you - a single purchase could transport you to every corner of the globe!

Chapter 2. Understanding Diversity: An Overview

Our world is an eye-catching spectrum of identities, languages, rituals, and traditions - each unique, robust, and each honing a crucial role in weaving the elaborate tapestry of our shared humanity. In the extensive scope of diversity that shapes our existence, each culture represents an indispensable strand - vibrant and vital, presenting an engaging narrative of human brilliance. This shared narrative's depth and vibrancy evolve commensurately with our understanding and acknowledgement of diversity, essentially seeping richness into our collective perspectives, behaviors, worldview, and general interaction with the world.

2.1. Unraveling the Concept of Diversity

Diversity, as a concept, is inherently dynamic and multi-layered, often encompassing aspects of race, ethnicity, gender, age, religion, ability, and socioeconomic status among other constructs. It hinges on the idea of 'difference', carving out its interpretation through observable and non-observable traits that distinguish one individual or group from another while mapping out a vast array of experiences, perceptions, values, skills, and worldviews. A key characteristic of diversity is its fluidity – diversity involves aspects that can be both fixed, such as biological traits, and fluid, such as culture, religion, or language, which can change depending on the surrounding context or personal development.

2.2. The Influence of Historical Timeline on Diversity Perspective

Historically, differing perspectives on diversity have been intricately woven into the fabric of humanity's timeline. From ancient Egyptian cosmopolitanism, where multiple ethnic groups co-existed and thrived, to the great Hellenistic cultures that valued diversity of thought and learning, and through to the modern-day increasingly globalized societies, views on diversity have shaped societies in varied ways.

However, the understanding of diversity was not always positive. There were, and still are, periods when fear of the 'other' or the unknown led to endeavors of homogenization and assimilation, designed to suppress diversity in favor of mono-culturalism. Nevertheless, in acknowledging these dark times, we also recognize the indomitable human spirit's capacity for growth, evolution, and ultimately, for harnessing the power of diversity for societal progress.

2.3. Diversity as a Catalyst of Innovation

Powerful insights unfurl when we perceive diversity as not merely a token demographic metric but a dynamic aspect of human interaction. It transforms into a catalyst, a force that drives innovation, creativity, and progress. The richness of diversity paves the way for a broader range of solutions to problems, encourages critical thinking, and engenders a deeper level of collective learning and understanding at both micro and macro levels.

Take, for instance, the field of technology. The influx of varied perspectives from diverse contributors has caused exponential advancements and breakthroughs, enhancing our lives tremendously. From varied coding languages to ever-evolving AI applications, the impact of diversity remains evident and impactful.

2.4. Diversity and Globalization: A Confluence of Cultures

Globalization further amplifies the impact of diversity. Shrinking geographical and cultural boundaries, faster and easier communication, increased mobility, and the broadening canvas of the digital era facilitate stronger interactions between countless cultures. This energetic cultural mix is encapsulated in the phrase 'global village', illuminating the paradoxes, dilemmas, and opportunities that diversity presents to modern society.

However, globalization also surfaces concerns of culture dilution. The accelerated merging of cultures might lead to a gradual homogenization process where smaller, niche cultures could lose their discrete elements, contributing to a rising 'global monoculture'. This potential loss heightens the importance of protecting and preserving cultural diversity.

2.5. The Future of Diversity: A Path Laid Ahead

As we move towards an increasingly connected world, understanding, acknowledging, and celebrating diversity will form an integral part of our global ethos. Cultivating a depth of appreciation for different cultures, languages, traditions, and perspectives will remain pivotal as we navigate the intricacies of a global society. This will not only help us safeguard the richness of our global cultural heritage but also foster a more harmonious, inclusive, and enriched global community.

In the end, empowerment through diversity stems from embracing 'differences' as a strength rather than viewing them through a lens of division. It is about understanding the 'other', about creating connections rather than erecting walls, and about cherishing the mosaic of human existence rather than the monotony of uniformity. As we delve into the chapters of this cultural odyssey, let's remember that each culture we encounter is not an isolated entity, but a vital brushstroke in the world's vibrant canvas. Through our shared journey, we aspire to learn, understand, value, and celebrate this beautiful dance of diversity.

Thus, we embark on this intellectual expedition across continents, exploring the intrinsic beauty residing in the heart of cultural diversity - each stop providing an eloquent testament to the strength, resilience, and creativity of mankind. Keep your mind open and your spirit engaged as we step into the vibrant world of global diversity.

Chapter 3. Africa's Rich Tapestry: Lessons in Unity and Resilience

Dive into the heart of Africa to witness an astounding display of unity, resilience, and the rich threadwork of shared traditions. Storied pasts weave across the continent, shaping the societal tapestry and leaving their profound imprints on various cultures. Africa remains a splendid charter of age-old traditions, urban trends, diverse languages, melodious music, culinary diversity, and arts that narrate an equally captivating and enriching tale of unity in diversity.

3.1. Understanding Africa's Diversity

Africa is a vast continent encompassing 54 countries, each teeming with unique people groups - from the cosmopolitan streets of Johannesburg to the Maasai tribes seamlessly merging the modern and traditional worlds. We indeed meet multiculturalism at its finest here, a beautiful dance of variations played out against the backdrop of shared continental pride.

More than 2000 distinct languages are spoken across the breadth and length of this continent. This linguistic variety is a testament to Africa's rich cultural heritage. These languages are not just communication tools; they carry customs, belief systems, oral traditions, and histories, ensuring their survival and continuity.

3.2. African Values that Unify the Continent

Cultural diversity notwithstanding, there is an overarching framework of values influencing African life - the concepts of Ubuntu and Harambee. Ubuntu, a Zulu term, is a philosophy promoting common humanity and interconnectedness. Derived from the Xhosa proverb *"Umuntu ngumuntu ngabantu"*, meaning 'a person is a person through other people', it emphasizes communal existence over individualism. Harambee, a Swahili word for 'pulling together', resonates with a similar ethos, advocating unity and collective development. These values provide a remarkable illustration of resonating principles that bind diverse African cultures together.

3.3. Resilience: The Backbone of Africa

Also noteworthy is African resilience, a spirit born of adversity but defiant in the face of it. The African narrative is dotted with tales of overcoming political turmoil, economic hardship, and social injustices. This resilient spirit manifests itself in varied ways, through the continent's fight for independence, overcoming colonial boundaries, to the modern-day struggles of combating poverty and disease. It is painted onto the hard-working faces of the people who wake each day to contribute to a greater future Africa dreams of and deserves.

3.4. African Music and Dance: Threads in the Tapestry

Every culture bears unique melodies, percussive rhythms, and dances that pulsate with the joy, sorrow, and spirit of their people.

African music symbolizes unity, expresses societal narratives, and germinates resilience. Through the Djembe drums' pulsing rhythms in West Africa to the Rainbow Nation's soulful isicathamiya, music imprinted with the stamp of African culture is a source of identity and continuity.

3.5. A Tapestry of Traditions, Influences, and Trends

Irrespective of the varied mosaic of traditions, Africa manages to encompass change while preserving its unique cultures within an urban-modern context. Global influences merge with native customs, birthing hybrid models that are contemporary yet deeply rooted in tradition. With these interwoven threads of past and present, Africa's strong cultural structures succeed dynamically in adapting and evolving to shape its future.

3.6. Africa: Lessons for the World

African unity, resilience, and cultural richness teach valuable lessons of coexistence, adaptability, and endurance. Although diverse in numerous locales, languages, and lifestyles, Africa unifies under shared values and a common spirit that can inspire global societies. In acknowledging and celebrating this diversity, the world has an opportunity to resonate with the profound wisdom that echoes from Africa, reinforcing the belief that our collective strength indeed lies in our diversity.

From Africa, we learn the power of community rekindled in the philosophy of Ubuntu, the strength of resilience as an adaptive response to adversity, and the power of music and dance as unifying forces that transcend barriers. These elements originate from this bountiful continent and serve as a poignant reminder of the human capacity to strive continuously for unity and harmony amidst diversity.

In conclusion, the African tapestry reveals intertwining threads of harmony embedded within the continent's contrasting cultures. It's a testament to the shared human spirit that thrives despite differences and adversities, drives the pursuit of common goals, and resounds the potent narrative of unity in diversity. This chapter beckons to all keen observers of human resilience and potential, for there is much to learn from the rich tapestry that is Africa.

Chapter 4. Crossing the Silk Road: The Harmonic Duality of Asian Cultures

As we embark on the journey down the fabled Silk Road, the expanse of diverse Asian cultures unfolds before us like an elaborate fan. The road, indeed, is long, and the landscapes are ever-changing, from the snow-white plateaus of Tibet to the sun-dappled bamboo forests of Japan. Our guide through this intricate maze of cultures is not a tangible path, but an intangible streak of the human spirit - the harmonic duality that sings at the heart of Asia, the sense of finding balance and harmony in the midst of contrasting aspects of life.

4.1. The Harmonic Landscape of China

We begin in the Middle Kingdom, the cradle of one of the oldest civilizations on earth. China is a paradigmatic symphony of yin and yang, symbolizing the balance of opposites, a harmonious coexistence of dualities. From the towering skyscrapers of Shanghai that jut out into the modern world, to the ancient clay terracotta regiments that stand guard in the mausoleums of ancient emperors, China is a living testament to harmony formed through contrasts.

But the duality is not confined to the physical realm. The spiritual landscape of the people here honours both ancestor veneration, the practice of bestowing respect on those who came before us, and the living moment in the form of Zen Buddhism, embodying the wisdom of recognizing the reality of the present. This rich mix of reverence for history and simultaneous commitment to the moment is a characteristic trait of Chinese culture, providing a unique harmony that allows both past and present to cohabitate.

4.2. A Spiritual Interlude: Buddhism and Hinduism

Asia, as the birthplace of many religions, illustrates spiritual duality. Predominant among this is the dialogue between Buddhism and Hinduism - two major religions spread across multiple nations, influencing and coexisting in a pan-Asian cultural sphere. They have shaped societies, histories, politics, and art across the continent, and often exist side by side within the same communities.

Buddhism, with its emphasis on introspection, acceptance, and mindfulness of the immediate reality, encourages followers to break away from desires and illusions. At the same time, Hinduism's world revolves around concepts such as Dharma (Moral law), Artha (prosperity), Kama (pleasure), and Moksha (liberation), creating a comprehensive framework for life and beyond. This coexistence without eliminating the other stands out, illustrating the depth of tolerance and cultural blend in Asian societies.

4.3. The Janus Face of Japan

Japan's culture is another fine example of duality and harmonious balance. The fast-paced urban life in cities like Tokyo, with a dizzying array of neon lights and fast trains, creates a striking contrast to the serene and cyclical rhythms of rural Japan, characterized by tranquil tea ceremonies and the Zen-like tranquility of rock gardens.

Japan's deep respect for nature, encapsulated in Shinto beliefs, blends well with Buddhism's life philosophy. An individual may visit a Shinto shrine for a wedding and a Buddhist temple for a funeral, and participate in both New Year's Eve bell-ringing and Cherry Blossom viewing. The duality here is not merely in complimentary opposites, but also how it creates room for internal paradoxes and contradictions, showing that harmony can involve a deep, intricate balance, rather than merely a simple binary.

4.4. Contrasting Colors of India

The Indian subcontinent, home to a diverse platter of cultures and religions,, also paints a picture of vibrant diversity. A realm where multilingualism is the norm, where countless religions interweave, this is truly a tapestry of contrast.

Yet at heart, the fabric of Indian society celebrates unity in diversity. Festivals such as Diwali, Holi, Eid, and Christmas find a common celebratory spirit across the country, each marking the calendar with their unique colors.

While the heart beats to the rhythmic tabla and the feet sway to the beats of dholak, the mind finds solace in the meditative chants of Vedas or the soulful Sufi melodies, exemplifying the country's profound cultural duality. Architecture in India mirrors this spirit: Mughal minarets coexist with Hindu temple spires, Catholic cathedrals with Jain shrines.

4.5. A Potpourri of Asian Cultures

Beyond the significant nodes of China, Japan, and India, the Asian expanse hosts a motley collection of cultures. Whether it's the Shamanistic practices in Mongolia, the blend of Hindu-Buddhist-Animist traditions of Southeast Asia, or the ancient Zoroastrian links in Persia, all contribute to the rich duality one finds across Asia.

The concept of coexistence and blend is central to many of these societies - the distinct flavors of Turkish tea are as much a part of their culture as the thousand-year-old Hagia Sophia striding the border between Christian and Islamic influences for centuries, standing as a testament to time.

The harmony of Asian culture lies in its people's DNA - a diverse array of histories, faiths, languages, cuisines, and yet, remarkably interconnected. With one foot poised in history and the other striding towards the future, it's this captivating dance of dualities that keeps the heart of Asia beating in a rhythm like no other. As we continue our journey, we allow the multitude of lessons from the old continent to seep into us - lessons of balance, of harmony, of welcoming contrasts - further weaving the colorful tapestry of our shared human tapestry. From our exploration, it becomes clear that the sprawling continent of Asia encapsulates a duality of existences, standing as a beacon of coexistence and mutual celebration, showing us that beautiful results can manifest from harmonious divergence.

Chapter 5. European Mosaic: Contrasts and Common Grounds

Indeed, Europe is more than just a geographic entity, but a vibrant mosaic of diversity, rife with a multitude of languages, cultures, political systems, and histories that color the landscape from Ireland in the West to Russia in the East, from the Nordic nations in the North to the sun-soaked Mediterranean regions in the South. From these contrasting characteristics are to be found not only the uniqueness of each culture but also the fascinating common grounds that unite this complex and varied continent.

5.1. The Cultural Spectrum and Shared Heritage

The cultural spectrum of Europe is widely diverse, extending from the Gaelic traditions in Ireland to Turkic influences in Eastern Europe. The deep-rooted histories and vibrant cultures that constitute the European continent vary extremely from one region to another. Yet, throughout the vast mosaic of peoples and traditions, European countries share some unifying elements.

An overarching common foundation lies in the continent's shared historical narrative shaped by major events like the Renaissance, Enlightenment, and the two World Wars, which had significant international repercussions. These immensely transformative periods had impact at every level of society and still echo in the collective consciousness. This shared history forms part of Europe's collective identity and unity amidst diversity.

Moreover, the shared heritage suggests a common lineage drawn from the great civilizations that once graced the European continent. These include the Greek, Roman, and Byzantine empires, followed by the vast network of the Frankish Kingdom and later the Holy Roman Empire. Ancient remnants still dot the landscape, and the longtime influence of these societies on law, language, architecture, and other cultural elements is hard to overlook.

5.2. Linguistic Diversity and Common Linguistic Roots

In the realm of language, Europe manages to accommodate over 200 vernaculars within its bounds, presenting an impressive panoply of linguistic diversity. Distinct languages like Finnish, Basque, and Hungarian stand apart from the Indo-European family, ladling out further intrigue into the continent's linguistic broth.

However, most European languages can be traced back to the Indo-European family, creating a layer of commonality beneath the apparent disparity. It is indeed fascinating to observe the cross-pollination of words and grammar rules among the Romance, Germanic, and Slavic buckets, all harking back to common ancestral roots.

5.3. Socio-Political Contrasts and the European Union

Politically, European nations exhibit a wide array of governance models ranging from parliamentary to presidential systems, and political ideologies that extend from social-democratic to conservative. Despite their striking differences, the sovereign nations have learnt to cooperate and even surrender a degree of sovereignty for a greater common good, as illustrated by the European Union (EU).

The EU is perhaps the most resonant symbol of Europe's quest for common grounds amidst contrasts. Signifying an unprecedented experiment in supranational governance, the EU embodies an ambitious endeavor to legally, economically, and politically unite a continent scarred by centuries of warfare.

5.4. Religion: Diversity and Shared Philosophical Underpinnings

Europe's religious landscape is as varied as its geographic contours, hosting a variety of Christian sects, alongside substantial communities of Muslims, Jews, Buddhists, Hindus, and those adhering to neopagan and secular philosophies. In the midst of this variety, Christianity, predominantly Catholicism, Orthodoxy, and Protestantism, has influenced European thought, art, culture, and politics for almost two millennia.

Certain philosophical principles common to all major European religions, such as the Golden Rule and ideals of compassion, though expressed differently, facilitate communication and understanding between them. Despite superficial deviations, these shared underpinnings offer an avenue to mutual respect, fostering an environment that encourages productive interfaith dialogue.

5.5. Conclusion: Harmony in Diversity

In conclusion, Europe is indeed a fascinating kaleidoscope of contrasts, yet marked by significant common grounds. Its diversity enriches the continent while the shared heritage, linguistic roots, strategic alliances, and philosophical underpinnings provide the tapestry with a sense of unity. Europe's story is an affirmation that while diversity may present challenges, it can also be a source of strength and vibrancy, an epitome of harmony in diversity.

Chapter 6. South America: Rhythms of Nature, Life, and Culture

As we travel southward to an area often referred as the "geographical mirror to the Northern Hemisphere", South America - a lively kaleidoscope of natural wonders, rhythmic life, and vibrant cultures, greets us. This chapter unfurls an exploration into this enchanting landscape, where we will dance to the pulsating tunes of Samba, navigate through the dense thickness of the Amazon Rainforest, and indulge in Andean traditions rooted in the sacred bonds of community and environment.

6.1. South America's Natural Canvas

South America's geographical vastness endows it with an impressive array of natural wonders. The Amazon Rainforest, the world's largest tropical rainforest, forms the very heartbeat of this region. With its astounding variety of flora and fauna, this place serves as a testament to the power of nature. It hosts millions of insect species, tens of thousands of plants, and nearly 2,500 different birds and mammals. The region also houses the fascinating Galapagos Islands, an archipelago teeming with unique species, which had famously inspired Darwin's theory of natural selection.

Patagonia, with its wilderness landscape, houses the Andes Mountains - the longest continental mountain range in the world, where regal condors glide above the snow-clad peaks, pumas tread around the glacial lakes, and sea lions bask on the icy shores. The Atacama Desert, one of the driest places on Earth, makes for a stark contrast with its lunar landscapes and salt lakes, but still teeming with life adapted to extreme conditions. This diversity affirms the resilience and adaptability of life, showcasing the amazing variety that the globe holds within its folds.

6.2. The Vibrant Pulse of Cultural Life

South America's vibrant culture is palpable in the rhythmic beats of its music, the colorful motifs of its textiles, and the lively banter in its dynamic markets. Whether its the energetic moves of Brazilian Samba, the heartfelt melodies of Argentine Tango, or the indigenous rhythmic beats reverberating through the Andes, the region's musical and dance traditions serve as a shared heartbeat of the populace, uniting diverse communities across geographical divides.

The region's rich indigenous heritage, evident in the Kuna people's molas (intricately sewn textiles) or the Quechuan pottery and weaving traditions, speaks volumes about the local's deep-rooted respect for nature and a profound sense of community. These traditions, passed down through generations, serve not just as an art form, but a means to preserve historical narratives and cultural identity.

6.3. Traditional Knowledge and Practices

South America's indigenous people possess a rich store of knowledge passed down through oral tradition. Ayahuasca ceremonies among the tribes of the Amazon, for instance, exhibit their deep spiritual connection with nature. This psychoactive brew, intended for healing and spiritual awakening, is reflective of the wisdom these tribes have gained through coexisting with the wilderness for centuries.

The Andean concept of 'ayni', which can loosely be translated to 'sacred reciprocity', dictates that one must give back to the nature and community in equal measure as one takes, illustrating a harmonious, sustainable model of living. Our travels through these lands not only offer insights into ancient wisdom but also illuminate pathways towards sustainable living.

6.4. The Fiesta of Flavors

South American cuisine also presents a feast of diverse flavors. From the traditional Peruvian Ceviche, where fresh fish is cured in citrus juices, to the savory aroma of Argentinian Asado (barbecue), the delicacies of this region tell stories of cultural assimilation and adaptability over centuries. The Chilean Curanto, a dish originally cooked in a pit, showcases how indigenous cooking techniques have evolved while retaining their core essence.

6.5. Pathway to Harmony: Cultural Lessons from South America

In the light of modernity, South America stands ahead in its ability to protect and promote cultural diversity. Despite the pressures of global homogenization, it retains an enchanting aura of tradition and identity, ever-resilient in its dance with globalization.

Lest we forget, the very soul of South America lies in its indigenous roots. The communal harmony prevalent among the Quechua-speaking people in the steep slopes of the Andes, the rituals surrounding the plant medicines in the secluded Amazonian tribes, or the Mapuche people's resistance against invaders to protect their lands, all offer profound lessons to the wider world. Here we learn about sustainable living, the value of community, and the ethos of resilience, all nestled within a culture that embraces and evolves with time.

This journey across South America leaves us in awe of its natural grandeur, enchants us with its rhythmic vitality, and enlightens us with its ancient wisdom. As we marvel at its vibrancy and diversity, we come to understand that the rhythms of nature, life, and culture are intertwined in a symphony of mutual respect and shared survival. At the end of our journey, we are left with an indelible footprint on our hearts, our minds awakened to the harmony that emerges from embracing diversity.

Chapter 7. North America's Melting Pot: A Celebration of Inclusivity

North America, a vibrant melting pot of rich cultures, is characterized by its diverse ethnic makeup, where individuals from various backgrounds coexist and share their traditions and values, thus fostering a spirit of inclusivity and unity in diversity.

7.1. Founding Cultures and Indigenous Tribes

Unfolding the tale of North America's multiculturism, we find it harmoniously straddling its indigenous roots and immigrant identities. Aboriginal cultures, including the Iroquois Confederation in the East, the Plains Indians in the Midwest, and the Navajo and Hopi tribes in the Southwest, established robust societal structures, sophisticated arts, spiritual customs, and adept survival strategies suited to the region's diverse landscapes. These communities continue to preserve their heritage, often through oral traditions, festivals, and practices, offering outstanding examples of resilience and adaptability.

7.2. Waves of Immigration: A Historical Overview

The intricate story of North America was rewritten with the arrival of European colonizers, initiating a tumultuous era of contact and escalation. Spaniards in the South, French in the North, and the British along the Atlantic coast brought not only a wave of socio-political change, but an infusion of artistic, culinary, architectural, and linguistic impressions that began to shape the continent's identity.

Subsequent waves of immigration from countries worldwide, particularly from Europe, Asia, Africa, and Latin America across the centuries, added layers to the cultural mosaic. Aiming for better lives, migrants brought their traditions, foods, languages, music, religions, and philosophies which they sought to preserve whilst adapting to the 'New World' dynamics.

7.3. Cultural Fusion and Assimilation

The phenomenon of cultural fusion embodies the North American essence, forming unique hybrid identities that influence popular global culture. Exemplifying this are food and music. Tacos have obtained a distinctly American touch, just as jazz, born from African rhythms and European harmonies, took on a new soul in the southern United States.

Concurrently, communities have faced struggles with assimilation, managing to retain distinct identities, such as the Amish, the Hasidic Jews, or the multicultural boroughs of big cities like New York and Toronto.

7.4. Inclusive Policy: The Melting Pot Ideology

North American nations, especially the United States and Canada, have also played an instrumental role in fostering inclusivity through policy. Envisaged as 'melting pots', they extol acceptance and assimilation of all ethnicities and cultures.

Canada's Multiculturalism Act of 1988 recognized and protected its cultural diversity at the legislative level. Similarly, the United States has grappled with its tumultuous history of racial tension to emerge with civil rights movements that champion equality. These strides in policy reflect the continent's strive to cherish multiculturalism and ensure fairness and justice.

7.5. Shared Practices, Shared Stories

Amidst diversity, elements of shared culture and universality exist. Holidays such as Thanksgiving in the United States and Canada illustrate cross-cultural fusion, with ancestral and immigrant narratives interweaving into a shared chronicle of gratitude. Sports, particularly soccer in Mexico and American football in the United States, serve as binding forces, transcending cultural lines and uniting communities in shared passion.

7.6. Diverse Landscapes, Diverse Lives

Paralleling the cultural diversity is North America's varied geography: from the ice-clad expanse of the Arctic to the sun-drenched beaches of California and Florida, from the urban skyline of Manhattan to the rustic charm of New England, and the vast wilderness of the Canadian Rockies to Mexico's arid deserts and lush rainforests. These contrasting landscapes define local customs and ways of life, creating a dynamic interplay between human societies and nature.

7.7. Towards a Prosperous Future of Inclusivity

Anticipating North America's cultural future highlights challenges, such as simmering racial tensions, immigration debates, and identity politics. However, positive developments, such as widening cultural awareness, growing acceptance of diverse identities, and progressive policies, suggest a hopeful trajectory towards a society that truly celebrates its diversity.

Evolving North America's cultural tapestry encapsulates the celebration of inclusivity in its rich history, vibrant present, and promising future, echoing the vitality of unity in diversity. It stands as a testament to our shared humanity, with each thread of unique heritage confirming that a single melody can inspire, but a symphony of cultures reverberates with resounding resonance.

Chapter 8. Oceanian Odyssey: Ancient Traditions, Modern Harmonies

"In the beginning, there was the Dreamtime…"

That's how an Aboriginal creation story begins, signifying the ancient roots of the cultures that palimpsest the Oceanian landscapes. From its golden beaches to verdant rainforests, from harsh outbacks to serene reefs, Oceania sings songs of ancient traditions and modern harmonies. The region's rich cultural tapestry, a blend of indigenous customs and contemporary transformations, contributes an invaluable thread to our complex global quilt of diversity.

8.1. The Aboriginal Dreaming: An Intricate Cosmology

"The Dreaming" or "the Dreamtime" lies at the heart of the spiritual belief and cosmology of Australia's indigenous communities - a belief system both profoundly complex and bewitchingly beautiful. Understanding this system opens avenues to a richer comprehension of Aboriginal continuity, identity, and their intricate relationship with the land. The Dreaming houses innumerable stories, explaining everything from the creation of landscapes, the fluctuations of the weather, to the behavioral patterns of plants and animals. Its monuments are dotted across Australia in a network of sacred sites – offering not just spiritual sustenance, but practical survival strategies coded into lore and landscape. Through creating the environment, the Dreaming also dictates how humans must live, generating a circular symbiosis between the tangible and intangible, physical and spiritual.

8.2. Pasifika Perspectives: A Tapestry of Fluid Identities

Moving eastward, we encounter the rich cultural domain of the Pasifika peoples - indigenous inhabitants of the myriad islands scattered across the South Pacific Ocean. A fascinating aspect of Pasifika cultures is their approach toward identities, fluid and constantly shifting, informed by the ever-changing ocean waves that surround them. They view identity as an ongoing process, a lifelong voyage fortified by their ancestors' wisdom and guided by their own experiences. This cultural understanding challenges often linear Western notions of identity and offers a broader perspective that accommodates continual shifts and transformations.

8.3. Maori Whakapapa: Roots, Relationships, and Respect

In the Maori culture of Aotearoa (New Zealand), one finds a dynamic demonstration of an explicit and respectful sense of ancestry and kinship, embodied in the concept of "whakapapa". A form of genealogy, whakapapa is more than just a family tree. It outlines a complete relational matrix, knitting together a network of relations not only within the human community but extending to the world of flora and fauna as well. It's a relationship that binds them via a shared genealogical spirit, a manifestation of their unified creation and existence.

8.4. Contemporary Oceania: The Modern-Day Harmony

Modern Oceania stands today as a testimony to this harmonious coexistence of ancient traditions and new-age ideologies. As an example, take the Aboriginal concept of "caring for country", which marries traditional land management practices with contemporary conservation science in Australia. The Pacific Islands, despite colonial influences, maintain their time-honored traditions, arts, and music, even as they adapt to the challenges posed by climate change and evolving socio-political landscapes.

8.5. Lessons from Oceania: Treading the Old and the New

Oceanian cultures illuminate our path forward in myriad ways by providing lessons in adaptability, interconnectedness, and respect for our natural world. They teach us that at the core of every successful society lies a healthy symbiosis between tradition and progress. However, these lessons also serve as a cautionary tale; the resilience of these cultures and their environments is now severely threatened by climate change and other external pressures. As we strive for global leadership and collaboration that values diversity, we must ensure that the collective wisdom of places like Oceania remains vibrant and intact as part of our shared cultural heritage.

The Oceanian odyssey is a rich illustrative journey into the beautiful amalgamation of old wisdom and new perspectives. A quintessential part of this human saga, it epitomizes the phrase "ancient traditions, modern harmonies", offering significant lessons for an increasingly connected world, echoing its unambiguous message - celebrate our past while embracing our future.

Chapter 9. Middle Eastern Mélange: A Confluence of Ancient Cultures

The middle east, colloquially known as the cradle of civilization, is a rich tapestry woven with deeply ingrained cultures, millennial-old histories, diverse beliefs, and ancient traditions. This chapter explores the profundity and rich variety of this ancient confluence, delving deep into this region that gave birth to some of the world's earliest civilizations and multitudes of cultural norms, spiritual beliefs, and intellectual advances.

9.1. Society and Norms in the Middle East

The societies in the Middle East are characterized by their diverse ethnicity and religious beliefs, punctuated by socialism, various cultural norms, and traditional laws. Bedouin culture, which honors hospitality and loyalty, is an example par excellence. Their societal structure, informed by the harsh realities of a nomadic lifestyle, calls for the tight-knit unity of a tribe with Bedouin tents, or "beit al-sha'ar," serving as centers for communal gatherings.

On the other hand, the family unit in more urban settings, whilst also deeply rooted in social and religious beliefs, is composed of hierarchical structures and roles. Respect for elders is universal and considered a moral obligation, ensuing from the wisdom they have acquired through the passing years.

9.2. Religion and Spirituality

The Middle East is the spiritual crucible of the world's three monotheistic religions: Judaism, Christianity, and Islam, providing a veritable plethora of spiritual and religious wisdom. Islam, in particular, governs the socio-cultural landscape of most Middle Eastern nations. The Five Pillars of Islam - Shahadah (faith), Salah (prayer), Zakat (charity), Sawm (fasting), and Hajj (pilgrimage) - reinforce the principles of social justice, community, and spirituality, deeply entwined with daily life.

While the focus often lies on Islam, it is important to remember the Jewish faith's rich history in places such as Israel and the Christian populations that inhabit lands from Lebanon to Egypt. Thus, each religion has left an indelible imprint on the region's cultural, social, and architectural landscape.

9.3. Cultural Achievements and Contributions

Notable among the epic narratives of the Middle East are its distinct contributions to science, arts, literature, and architecture. The Golden Age of Islam, spanning the 8th to the 14th century, was a period where science, philosophy, medicine, and education flourished. Libraries, like the House of Wisdom in Baghdad, became the beating heart of this intellectual renaissance, leading to breakthroughs in astronomy, mathematics, and medicine.

In literature, the Middle East has been the birthplace of many written masterpieces such as The Epic of Gilgamesh, The Arabian Nights, and eloquent poetry collections from legendary poets like Rumi and Hafez. The singular tradition of oral storytelling maintains a vibrant presence, with the grandeur of history and metaphorical depth encapsulated in the rhyme and rhythm of every verse or tale.

Architecturally, the Middle East is a mesmerizing blend of ancient and modern structures. From the Pyramids of Egypt, the ancient city of Petra, to the modern marvel of Burj Khalifa, this region has consistently shaped mankind's structural imagination and left its mark on skylines worldwide.

9.4. Middle Eastern Cuisine: A Feast of Diverse Flavors

Middle Eastern cuisine is warmly embraced around the globe for its fragrant blend of spices, diverse ingredients and rich flavors. From the smoky eggplant dip baba ghanoush, sizzling kebabs, creamy hummus to the sweet pastry baklava, every dish is a celebration of tradition and a testament to the region's rich agricultural history. Food in the Middle East is not merely sustenance. More so, it is an experience, a cherished time for family gatherings, steeped in age-old rituals, seasoned stories, and the warmth of shared meals.

9.5. Cultural Celebrations and Festivals

The Middle East observes many spiritual and cultural festivals, imbued with deeply rooted traditions. In the Islamic calendar, Ramadan, the holy month of fasting, exhibits a profound sense of communal experience. Eid Al-Fitr and Eid Al-Adha are occasions of joyous gatherings, charity, and feasting. Mawlid, the birth of Prophet Muhammad, is also fervently celebrated.

All of these cultural components come alive in every corner of the Middle East, in every souk or bazaar, every mosque or church, in every verse of a poem or the lines of a heartfelt story, in the captivating texture of ancient ruins and sparkling facades of towering skyscrapers. This confluence of diverse, ancient cultures paints a tantalizing and deeply enriching picture of a region that has been, and continues to be, a profound contributor to global cultural heritage.

Chapter 10. Lessons, Reflections, and Inspirations: A Cross-Cultural Comparative Analysis

As we embark on this illuminative journey, delving deep into the various cultural tenets, practices, and paraditudes, we are instantly treated to an enchanting potpourri of vibrant customs, rich histories, and unique sociopolitical structures that do not just signify the distinctness of the cultures we've traversed, but also, emphatically represent the convoluted interweave of human society. This chapter aims at sifting through the intricate web of cultural diversities to unravel the concurrent themes that course through them, elucidating the invaluable lessons each bears, how they reflect on collective human experience, and how their inspirational elements can be harnessed for a more cohesive and symbiotic global society.

10.1. Threads of Commonality: Nations Apart, Hearts Unified

Interestingly, despite the apparent disparities, deep-rooted elements of unity thread through each culture. Our sojourn through the tribal settlements of Africa, the expansive plains of North America, and the sprawling urban lunacies of Europe, subtly but surely, brought forth this truth. Whilst the African cultures showcased a deeply ingrained sense of community binding, tenets of communal help and cooperation emerging as dominant themes, a similar vein throbbed within the European cultures - albeit flavored with individualistic undertones - where bonds of shared history, food, and language provided a strong sense of cultural cohesion. The communal celebrations in South America, with their heartfelt renditions of folklore and tales, further reinforced this universal thread of collective identity and communion weaving through disparate cultures.

10.2. Resilience and Adaptability: Life's Constant Companions

Resilience and adaptability presented themselves as other globally pervasive themes. Tracing the journey of the Silk Road, we internalized the adaptive brilliance of the Asian cultures; their ability to harmonize with the changing geopolitics, environments, and dynamics, signifying the unyielding wheels of human adaptability and resilience. The Inuit people's survival in harsh Arctic conditions, their practice of hunting, their shelter-building skills, and their ability to utilize scant resources exemplify resilience in its purest form. Incidentally, this theme also runs rampant through African, European, South American, and Oceanian cultural narratives - the common chords interlinked, ever-present, undeterred by borders or geographical locations.

10.3. The Role of Art and Creativity: A Reflection of Humanities in Full Bloom

Art and creativity, another relentless accompaniment of human expression, found ubiquity unsurprisingly. The Masai dance, the Native American dreamcatchers, the elegantly adorned markets of Marrakech, the oriental charm of Kyoto's temples; all bespoke of the beautiful symphony of human artistry and creativity. Art, thus, becomes the mirror to societal values, historical legacies, and emotional landscapes across cultures, its diversity enhancing its universal appeal.

10.4. Variation and Unity in Spiritual Practices

Permeating cultures and bridging humans universally is the domain of spirituality. Diverse spiritual practices, observed across continents and cultures, presented another mosaic of varied yet unified human experience. The tranquil Zen practices of the East, the mystical Sufi traditions of the Middle East, the shamanistic rites of the indigenous people of America and Oceania, the reverberating chants in the African plains, all emanated resonances that, while distinct, echoed a singular human quest for spiritual connection and transcendence.

After this comprehensive cultural exploration, we learn that cultures, though diverse, are rays of a human experience spectrum — variant and vibrant but emanating from the same source. They harbor lessons of unity, resilience, creativity, and spirituality that, once internalized, echo the universal human experience, enriching us as individuals and society. This global perspective can guide us in establishing harmony in our increasingly connected world, and holds key to honoring diversity and fostering unity in this ever-active global fraternity.

As we further nurture these lessons and reflections, our inspirations fuel the envisioning of a harmonious future. Embracing diversity, unifying through common threads, learning from each other, and adapting for collective growth – these are the cornerstones for nurturing global harmony, a harmony rooted deeply in the appreciation and celebration of human diversity.

Chapter 11. The Future of Global Harmony: Nurturing Diversity in an Increasingly Connected World

In this concluding chapter, we find ourselves standing at the precipice of a new age - an era defined increasingly by globalization and interconnectedness. As we enter this new epoch, it becomes more important than ever before to understand, appreciate, and champion the values of diversity and multiculturalism that add to the rich tapestry of humanity.

11.1. The Interconnected World

The advent of internet technology has undoubtedly brought about a metaphorical "shrinking" of our world. Information now travels at lightning speed, transcending geographical barriers and bringing diverse cultures and societies closer together than ever before. But as this technological revolution continues unabated, fundamental questions arise surrounding the preservation and celebration of cultural diversity within a rapidly homogenizing global society.

In the grand scheme of human history, the instantaneous global communication we experience today is a relatively new phenomenon. It is incredible to think how a message, an idea, or a request can be sent halfway across the globe in mere seconds, or how a video call can let us see and interact with someone despite thousands of miles separating us. These advancements have accelerated the pace at which we exchange thoughts, ideas, and innovations, allowing for a global dialogue and a cross-pollination of cultures like never before.

However, with this interconnectedness comes a worry: the worry of homogenization, the fear that our myriad cultures, with their unique customs, traditions, and perspectives, will be replaced by a uniform global culture. It's a concern that we must seriously address. But preserving and celebrating diversity within a unifying global culture is not a zero-sum game. Indeed, they complement and enhance each other.

11.2. Cultural Diversity in the Internet Era

The internet serves as both a powerful force for globalization and a vital tool for cultural preservation. On one hand, it presents a tempting tableau of Western or globalized culture that threatens to eclipse traditional customs and ways of life. On the other, its unmatched ability to share and preserve knowledge provides a valuable opportunity to celebrate, protect, and raise awareness of the world's diverse cultures.

So, how can we ensure that it is used to benefit all cultures equally?

Education is one answer. By leveraging digital platforms to share stories and educate young minds about the importance and value of their own cultures – as well as those of others – we can promote acceptance, tolerance, and mutual respect. This usefulness can extend to adults as well, providing easily accessible gateways to other cultures, stimulating curiosity, encouraging understanding, and fostering a deep appreciation for the richness of our diverse globe.

Moreover, digital platforms can democratize the sharing and preservation of culture. In the past, the task of preserving and disseminating cultural heritage often fell to anthropologists, historians, or culture specialists. However, the internet enables anyone with a data connection to become a custodian of their culture, adding their voice and perspective to the global conversation. The importance of this cannot be overstated in a world where many traditional ways of life are endangered.

11.3. Nurturing Global Harmony through Diversity

As we move further into this era of globalization, it becomes our shared responsibility to foster a sense of belonging within an increasingly diverse society. Every culture possesses its unique stories of struggle and triumph, idiosyncrasies, and invaluable wisdom. At their core, all of these packages of knowledge reflect a common human experience. Through sharing and appreciating these aspects of our collective heritage, we can foster empathy, understanding, and unity.

Embracing this diversity does not mean surrendering individual cultural identities; rather, it involves weaving these identities into the ever-evolving tapestry of global culture.

The way forward, therefore, must be approached with a conciliatory spirit. The goal isn't to create a world where everyone is the same, but rather one where differences are celebrated, where each group is given space and respect to contribute to a harmonious global society, a world where cultural pluralism thrives alongside global unity.

11.4. The Road Ahead

There is no doubt that we stand on the brink of a transformative era in human history. As we march further into the 21st Century and deeper into the Internet Age, we are being presented with an unprecedented opportunity to shape the future of human culture. The choices we make now about how we handle this rapid change will leave a lasting mark on generations to come.

The challenge we face is throwing into sharp relief the trade-offs between global coherence and preservation of cultural diversity but we must impress upon every heart the truth that these two are not irreconcilable. We must foster and nurture a conscious celebration of diversity, even as we move closer and closer together in this interconnected world.

In the end, we must remember that our common humanity does not lie in the homogenization of cultures, but rather in the harmony that comes from their diversity. By embracing and nurturing this harmony, we can foster a world that is deeply interconnected yet vibrantly diverse, giving birth to a truly global community. Together, we can build a world of unity, flourishing in diversity. A world connected, yet distinct. A world that continues its dance around the sublime medley of its many, beautiful cultures.